STEPHANIE ENNIS

CRAFTING

**The Ultimate Guide on How to Make a Living
From Crafting, Learn Different Arts and Crafts
That Can Help You Earn Cash**

Descrierea CIP a Bibliotecii Naţionale a României
STEPHANIE ENNIS
    CRAFTING. The Ultimate Guide on How to Make a Living From Crafting, Learn Different Arts and Crafts That Can Help You Earn Cash / Stephanie Ennis – Bucharest: Editura My Ebook, 2021
    ISBN

STEPHANIE ENNIS

CRAFTING

The Ultimate Guide on How to Make a Living From Crafting, Learn Different Arts and Crafts That Can Help You Earn Cash

My Ebook Publishing House
Bucharest, 2021

TABLE OF CONTENT

Introduction 7

Chapter 1: *Arts And Crafts Basics* 9

Chapter 2: *Main Types Of Crafts* 11

Chapter 3: *Creating A Concept* 13

Chapter 4: *Supplies And Skills* 16

Chapter 5: *Marketing For An Arts And Crafts* 18

Chapter 6: *Arts And Crafts Fairs* 20

Chapter 7: *Successful Business Mindset* 23

Chapter 8: *Candle Making Crafts* 25

Chapter 9: *Christmas Crafts for the Home* 28

Chapter 10: *Crafts That Work For Halloween* 32

Chapter 11: *Handmade Valentine's Day Crafts* ……….. 36

Wrapping Up …………………………………………... 39

INTRODUCTION

All types of leisure activities can be turned into a viable business should the individual decide to make it an income earning venture. With this in mind, anyone wanting to venture into the business field should be well equipped with the various connecting dos and don'ts of doing business. Get all the info you need here.

CHAPTER 1

ARTS AND CRAFTS BASICS

Synopsis

All crafts can and usually are categorized into a few major areas, which include paper crafts, textile based crafts, decorative crafts, and fashion focused crafts and crafts that also serve as functional piece. Besides these more obvious and areas there are also other lesser known yet fairly popular arts and crafts styles. Basically anything that has some features of being handmade can be classified under these categories.

The Basics

The following are some elements that can be connected to the arts and crafts business entity:

If the crafts business is to make an impact and produce the desired revenue then there should be a plan in place to eventually bring this to reality.

For some starting out on a part time basis is a better option that to go into it full time, as there is no assurance that the particular art or craft will be well received as a business entity.

Perhaps taking some lessons to fine tune the individual's capabilities would be a wise step to take if one is serious about converting the hobby to becoming an actual business.

These classes will help to expose the individual to elements that would perhaps not be already known thus creating the opportunity for the individual to be savvier when it comes to the art and craft work.

Part of the process for planning the business, should also include checking out the competition in the particular art and craft field the individual is intending to be a part of. Armed with this knowledge the individual will be able to decide if the choice made is the right one.

CHAPTER 2

MAIN TYPES OF CRAFTS

Synopsis

The arts and crafts field is quite vast and diversified, but it can be broken down into a few main areas based on the materials being used to create the intended item. Therefore if the individual is contemplating venturing into the arts and crafts business platform, some knowledge on the different types of crafts should be understood.

A Quick Look

The following is a short description of the main different areas that are usually associated with crafts:

Textile crafts – this type of craft would include the use of fabrics, yarn and any type of surface design which may include knitting, weaving, dyeing and appliqué. Although some of these end products can also be regarded as fashion crafts in it still basically textile based.

Paper crafts – as the name implies the basis of this craft is the use of paper to make the items. This is a very basic style craft and is usually introduced at a very young age which is usually as part of a classroom project.

It is mainly a favorite for children's' projects to be made as gifts and mementos. As for the more experienced creations the paper crafts would include paper mache, calligraphy and paper making. Certain wood engravings are sometimes categorized as paper crafts too.

Decorative crafts – this particular category does not really focus on the use of any particular material and is basically just creations that are meant to be appreciated as decorative items.

Anything from furniture to stained glass fixtures come under this very creative category, which normally requires a high amount of skilled labor.

Fashion crafts – for some this is the most popular and rewarding category to venture into as it involved the "dressing or decorating" of the human body as a palate. This area knows no bound in the name of creativity and individualism. It is also the most highly featured and prized category as fashion.

CHAPTER 3

CREATING A CONCEPT

Synopsis

This creation of concepts requires a little planning and thought. Previously the idea of creating a concept was usually done when the services of an advertising company was sought. However of late anyone and everyone intending to go into business, where the visibility element is pivotal and needed while maintaining the recognition in an individualistic way, the idea of concept creation becomes a vital.

Plan

The following are some points that can shed some ideas on the issue of concepts:

Concept ideas in the form of proposals – this is mostly where the consumers view are taken into consideration and any adjustments made to the business, products or service is very much dictated by the customers input.

The information can be gotten through the various different levels of the business engine and not necessarily only from the consumer. Any feedback that can be enlightening is highly valued.

Concept ideas selection process – here a whole bunch of ideas are discussed and categorized according to its merits and then the process of elimination begins where the eventual pick is imagined to be the best concept to go with.

This exercise usually involves the powers that be and all others who have important contributing thoughts on the eventual pick made.

Concept marketing strategy – at this point the concept becomes more detailed and a lot more thought and planning is exercised.

Mistakes or wrong assumptions made at this stage would not bear well on the overall success of the business endeavor as this planning stage is the backbone of eventual promotions tagged to the business engine.

Concept physical development and testing – this stage required the actual reaching out process where the target customer base is used as a guideline to gauge the eventual reception the business, product or service will receive. This exercise is usually carried out as a launching pad for the business.

CHAPTER 4

SUPPLIES AND SKILLS

Synopsis

Every business requires certain basic elements in order to ensure its success, and supplies and skill usually rank quite highly on the requirements platform. Therefore before the individual even decides to actually get into the serious procedures of starting up a business, there should be some basic understanding of the needs and importance of these two elements.

What You Need

Supplies will be the basis of the business to start with and without the supplies there really is no business to speak of. Getting all the information such as what is required and how this requirement can be fulfilled in a professional and timely manner is important to the eventual smooth running of the business engine.

There is also the need to look into the kind of supplies needed and whether there are any legal implications tagged to the use of such items.

If there is a need to get legal approval to use the item then the necessary documentations should be files with the relevant governing bodies before such item can be included for use in making the products intended.

If it is not possible to use such items based on the rejections of the governing bodies than immediate steps would be taken to find suitable alternative which are both acceptable and easy to acquire.

Skills are also another very important element that should get serious consideration when starting up the business endeavor. Art and crafts is nothing without the ever important presence of the skills element.

Not just anyone can churn out such items without the knowledge and skill it would have taken to master such a production.

Often this particular aspect is taken for granted and when the business starts to earn some serious revenue and there is a need to expand, not having the skilled labor to help churn out the necessary amounts to meet the demands will eventually jeopardize the entire business entity, causing the customers to look elsewhere to satisfy their needs.

CHAPTER 5

MARKETING FOR AN ARTS
AND CRAFTS BUSINESS

Synopsis

Marketing for arts and crafts is quite similar to marketing any other products with only a few distinctive different. These differences are due to the fact that the market for such items are quite niche and such items cannot be successfully touted by the masses as it lose its originality in the selling tactic.

Marketing

The following are some recommendations on how to understand and plan the marketing tactics for arts and crafts businesses:

Doing some research is the first thing to exercise in the quest to understand the market requirements of the time and the general likes and dislikes of the intended customer base.

18

With this in mind the individual intending to launch an art and craft business will be able to gauge if the intended product is suitable as a revenue earning tool or if there is a need to redesign or even rethink the entire concept of the item to be made for sales.

Pricing the items reasonable is also another marketing strategy that should be looked into. After the market research the individual should be able to gauge just how much a customer is willing to pay for such items.

Correct and compatible pricing is very important to ensure that the available market for the product in actually induced to making the product a revenue earning platform.

Marketing strategies that direct focus to the ideal pricing for the product, will successfully garner the desired interests which will lead to the desired [projected earnings.

Building a strong mailing list is also another effective marketing strategy when it comes to creating visibility and bringing the product to the customer. Making the customer aware of the existence of the item and creating the platform for easy and quick purchases to be made will encourage the intended customer base to excitedly make purchases.

CHAPTER 6

ARTS AND CRAFTS FAIRS

Synopsis

The main idea behind these arts and crafts fair is to being to attention the works of those participating in the exercise to the viewing public. However there are also many other reasons why this particular platform is both useful and exciting for those so inclined.

Fairs

The following are just some of the reasons why arts and crafts fairs have become very popular entities of late:

A lot of the participants of the arts and crafts fair get involved in this type of event for the convenience it facilitates. The locations and times chosen to organize such events are usually very convenient and timely.

Product exposure – this is a splendid platform to display the individual's creations with the sole intention of gaining revenue through the potential purchase of the items on display.

The fairs are usually organized periodically to ensure those in the industry have a suitable venue that is not exorbitantly costly to display their wares for business purposes.

The fairs are patronized by like minded individuals who share the same affinity to the products on display, thus making it an ideal one stop location to find anything and everything one may be looking for.

Buying opportunities – some of these fairs can also function as displaying platforms for future business opportunities. It is not uncommon for established business owners to browse through such fairs looking for opportunities to further expand their already successfully preexisting businesses.

Forming new partnerships and expansion programs can be quite common an exercise at an arts and crafts fair.

As most of the participants in such fairs are considered cottage industry style businesses, larger companies looking for new ideas also visit such fairs to form business liaisons which could be rather successful especially for the individual displaying specialized and unique style goods.

This becomes even more lucrative if the owner of the said item or design has had the foresight to have the elements patented.

CHAPTER 7

SUCCESSFUL BUSINESS MINDSET

Synopsis

The following are some tips on the successful business mindset that is well worth following in order to generate successful revenue earning possibilities:

Perhaps the most effective and motivating tool would be to actually visualize the business engine and its definite accompanying success. This is different from simply visualizing the possibilities, as this exercise requires the actual visualization of the already successful entity.

Keeping this visual picture prominent in the individual mind's eye, will help to ensure there are enough motivational thoughts and actions that will eventually contribute to the business success becoming a reality and no longer just a vision.

Maintaining a successful business mindset also requires the actual conscious effort made on the part of the potential business owner to avoid all contact with negative thinking individuals. By avoiding pessimistic people the new business owner will effectively keep possible negative thoughts at bay.

These negative elements can sometimes cause even the strongest and focused mindsets to stumble, thus avoidance is better than having to struggle with mostly unfounded doubts.

Being willing to make sacrifices when necessary is also another element that should be well understood by the new business owner.

Most successful entrepreneurs have attested to the fact that all initial sacrifices have proven to be well worth it in the long run.

This will help the individual refrain from feeling bitter from having to make such sacrifices. It will also help others around the individual; better understand the reasons for such commitment the individual is focused on simulating.

CHAPTER 8

CANDLE MAKING CRAFTS

Making your own candles is a favorite craft and hobby many individuals. They find the process to be enjoyable and relaxing. Candle makers have been know to turn to their hobby in times of stress. For some candle makers, once they learn the basics they are ready for new challenges. Purchasing books on candle making can provide you with everything from basic instructions, tips, and creative ideas to make beautiful candles. Most candle making books offer wonderful illustrations as well as step by step instructions.

The type of book you want to purchase will depend on your candle making experience, the types of candles you are interested in making, and if you are making candles for fun or to sell. Take the time to explore what each book has to offer you before making a purchase so that you won't be disappointed.

You might also check with your local library for books on candle making. If you find one there you really like then you have the option to purchase it. You can also find great discounts on used candle making books online at Ebay and Yahoo Auctions.

"The Candle Maker's Companion" by Betty Oppenheimer and Deborah Balmuth is considered to be the "must have" candle making book. It offers information for everyone including beginners and advanced. Another great choice is "The Encyclopedia of Candle Making Techniques". This book has gotten rave reviews for providing quality information in an easy to understand form.

For those of you who have a solid foundation of basic candle making processes, consider trying "The Complete Candle Maker Techniques, Projects, and Inspirations". The book offers great photos of forty different candles you can make. There are step by step instructions to help you make any of them that interest you. This book includes great tips and points as well to help candle makers avoid the common mistakes that affect the results of their candles.

For those of you who enjoy making candles for special occasions and holidays, the book "Creative Candles: Over 40 Inspiring Projects for Making and Decorating Candles for Every

Occasion" by Sue Spear is a great book to consider for your collection. This book features candle making ideas for Halloween, Easter, and Christmas. There are also ideas for creating candles to use as center pieces and for wedding decorations.

If you are interested in doing candle making with your children, "Great Candles" is especially designed with fun candles that are easy to do with them. The book is also written in a way that children will be interested in reading it as well. The internet is a great resource to find other great candle making books to meet your expectations.

Candle making is a great pastime. You can educate yourself on the areas of candle making by exploring various books. There are books designed for all candle making levels of expertise as well as on particular themes of candles and types of candles. The market is flooded with resources in the area of candle making, so the process of tracking down a few good books on the subject should be easy as well as fairly inexpensive. Remember to check the library, local book sales, and yard sales for these books as well. Compare prices online to make sure you get the best price for the ones you are interested in.

CHAPTER 9

CHRISTMAS CRAFTS FOR THE HOME

If you are in the crafting business Christmas is one of the best times of year to get your new product line out to your customers.

Christmas is the one time of year that most people pull out all the stops when it comes to decorating. There is no such thing in the eyes of many as excess and the one who gets started last is the one who often finishes last. Each year the displays, lights, and sounds grow larger and more complex. The problem is that most people cannot keep up with the newest, latest, and greatest in Christmas decorations. For these people there should be no worry. Christmas is a celebration of good will and not a competition to have the grandest display (at least that is what it should be).

Hopefully, the ideas below will help you enjoy decorating your home for Christmas once again as a passion for the holiday rather than a competition. The most important thing is that you choose Christmas decorations that have meaning to you rather than the decorations you feel your friends and family will like. Christmas is very personal and different to every person that celebrates the holiday. Not everyone that celebrates this particular holiday will celebrate in precisely the same way.

If the nativity scene is central to your Christmas celebration then by all means be sure to include it. You should not, however, feel compelled to include it if you have a more secular than religious view of the holiday. Angels are the same way though there are many who have little religious use for angels that still hold them in high regards as decorations around Christmas each year. Go with your preferences and convictions and you might find that the process is a joy rather than a chore.

I am a fan of Christmas decorations I love the blinking lights and the beauty of the greenery mixed with bright shades of red and gold. I love the fact that 200 houses can be decorated for Christmas inside and out and it is very unlikely that any two will look the same. I love the fact that for one month out of the year children are looking out their windows in awe at the bright lights and the cheery characters that light up the cold wintry rooftops all around.

If you are lost when it comes to decorating ideas of your own, my biggest suggestion is to pick what you like most about Christmas and choose your home decorating style around that one thing. As the years go by, inspiration strikes, and you find more things to like or dislike about Christmas your decorations can change accordingly. Perhaps the greatest thing about decorating your home for Christmas is that nothing is set in stone. If it worked last year, that doesn't mean it will work for this Christmas and there is no reason you should feel compelled to do it.

Some great ideas or themes for Christmas home decorating include the following: snow globes, cherubs, angels, Santa Clauses, snowmen, birds, candles, wreathes, and stockings. While this is by no means an exhaustive list of Christmas decorations it is a good place to start when ideas are needed. Favorites of my children include cartoon characters, gingerbread men, gingerbread houses, balls, grape clusters, and ribbons.

If you want to create a truly special style of home decorating for Christmas try a homemade Christmas. This means that all the ornaments, centerpieces, wreaths, garlands, and decorations are made by hand rather than purchased whole.

It will certainly make an impression on visitors and you and your family can enjoy the process of creating your very own Christmas decorations for the holiday season.

There are so many wonderful ideas, tips, and tricks when it comes to decorating your home for Christmas that it is incredibly difficult to point to one specific idea and say 'this is it'. However, finding a theme that speaks to your heart is what Christmas is all about. Well that and spending time with those who mean the most to you in the world.

CHAPTER 10

CRAFTS THAT WORK FOR HALLOWEEN

If there is ever a time of year when the ghosts and goblins roam the streets of the modern world, that time would be Halloween. Today's ghost and goblins are probably a little more frightening than at any other time in history but they are often tempered by a princess seeking frogs and a few witches and wizards along the way. Halloween is a great day to be a kid but can also be a great day for grown ups as well. Decorating for Halloween can be almost as fun as going out and begging for candy any day of the week.

Besides, having a well decorated home for this holiday gives you the perfect excuse to scare the evil out of some young ghoul or vampire that thinks he or she has the market cornered on frightening. The really cool thing about decorating for Halloween is that it is not one size fits all. You are perfectly free to find some very scary home decorations for this delightful holiday or take on a kinder, gentler, more kid friendly style of decorating. Either decision is yours and yours alone and should carefully monitor the scare-ability of your own children when deciding. You certainly don't want them afraid to come home.

For a more frightening Halloween scene you will probably want to use some strobe lights, frightening music and sound effects, dry ice in order to incorporate spooky fog, and plenty of spider web type netting in order to give those who dare approach your door bells a complete and thorough case of the willies. Doesn't this sound like so much fun? Coffins with headless straw men are also a great addition as well as skittering spiders and the occasional chainsaw or two. A glow in the dark hockey mask may also be a good choice. Bodiless heads suspended by fishing wire are also quite the highlight for a true and robust fright.

If your goal is to create a kid friendly Halloween atmosphere there are cheerful pumpkin decorations that can be found in many shapes and sizes as well as Casper the friendly ghost, Frankenstein piñatas, and countless other fun party favors that are designed to bring entertainment and delight rather than terror and far. String pumpkin lights around the porch for added lighting and another friendly face in addition to keeping plenty of candles and lanterns lit nearby. Not all trick or treaters are older kids who appreciate a good scare so keep this in mind as the little ghosts, goblins, princesses, and super heroes arrive.

For adult gatherings all bets are off when it comes to home decorating for Halloween. There are all kinds of themes that can be followed from the incredibly zany and outrageous to the frightening or flamboyant. The biggest suggestion in these matters is to have fun at all times and bring the be the life of the party rather than having the decorations upstage your efforts. Far too many people spend more time concerned with how they will decorate their homes rather than wondering how they will decorate themselves for the festivities. If you find the perfect costumes all eyes will be on you and not your decorations.

Favorite suggestions for adult parties would include strobe lights, much like the frightening scene described above, low additional lights, perhaps black lights near the food and drink area of the party. More dry ice (if tolerable some people have difficulties with the smell particularly those with allergies or asthma so you may want to avoid this inside your home and leave it for the exterior). Bales of hay in the corner make excellent additional seating and can contribute to the harvest/autumn/Halloween atmosphere you are attempting to create. Just remember that the underlying goal is for you and
34

your guests to have a great time. Have good food, good music, and good friends, and the decorations really and truly should be a secondary concern.

CHAPTER 11

HANDMADE VALENTINE'S DAY CRAFTS

Stores and florists spend a great deal of time, money and effort promoting their products as perfect for Valentine's Day. This is done for good reason as most people turn to commercially available products on Valentine's Day to give a great gift to their loved ones. However, with a little effort you may find you can give your partner a really great gift on Valentine's Day which comes straight from your heart. This can be done in the form of a homemade gift. Despite what you may be thinking it does not take a great deal of time or talent to make these great gifts. This article will provide a few ideas for homemade gifts you can give to your loved one on Valentine's Day.

A scrapbook is one of the most obvious homemade gifts you can give to your partner on Valentine's Day. It is also one of the easiest homemade gifts you can make and also one of the gifts which is most likely to be greatly appreciated by your partner. This is a great combination if you want to give your partner a spectacular gift on Valentine's Day. To make a great scrapbook start out by selecting the pictures you want to use in the scrapbook. You can select pictures of each of you individually, pictures of the two of you together, pictures of places the two of you have visited together or any combination of the pictures previously mentioned. Once you select a series of pictures you really like there will likely be an obvious theme for the scrapbook. Once this theme emerges you can search for the scrapbook as well as accessories for the scrapbook such as stickers, ribbons or other graphics. Finally, assembling the scrapbook is as easy as gluing the pictures and accessories to the page and putting everything together in an order which makes sense.

Homemade candles are another great gift you can give your partner for Valentine's Day. Making candles is actually quite simple. You can find kits in craft supply stores which will not only include everything you need to make a great candle or two but also provide you with simple step by step instructions on how to melt the wax, insert the wick, pour the candle and allow the candle to set before releasing it from the mold. Also, there will likely be the opportunity to use dyes and perfumes to create a candle of a customized color and scent. When adding color or scent to a candle, care should be taken to add the dye or perfume at the appropriate time for the best results.

One final idea for a homemade Valentine's Day gift is a CD filled with your partner's favorite music or a DVD with pictures of videos of the two of you together. You can even combine the videos with movie clips or music which you think fits well with the rest of the images or video. This may sound like it is extremely difficult but it really is not. With the technological advancements being made, many of us would be surprised to learn that we can do a lot of these things on our own computers at home. However, if you are having a great deal of trouble, you might want to consider consulting a friend or family member for advice on how to accomplish your goal. This way you can still give your loved one a homemade gift for Valentine's Day but you will have some help with the most difficult parts of the project.

WRAPPING UP

Starting any business usually has the same common goal, which is to make the business into a money making endeavor. Therefore in order to ensure this ideal scenario becomes a reality, there is a need to have the accompanying mindset that will keep the individual focused towards the end goal of creating a successful business entity.

.

Printed by Libri Plureos GmbH in Hamburg,
Germany